W9-CDX-931

Rookie
Read-About®
Dinosaurs

Oviraptor

by Wil Mara

Content Consultant
Gregory M. Erickson, PhD
Paleontologist
The Florida State University
Tallahassee, Florida

Reading Consultant
Jeanne Clidas
Reading Specialist

Children's Press®
An Imprint of Scholastic Inc.
New York Toronto London Auckland Sydney
Mexico City New Delhi Hong Kong
Danbury, Connecticut

Library of Congress Cataloging-in-Publication Data
Mara, Wil.
  Oviraptor/by Wil Mara.
    p. cm.—(Rookie read-about dinosaurs)
  Includes bibliographical references and index.
  ISBN-13: 978-0-531-20863-2 (lib. bdg.)   ISBN-10: 0-531-20863-X (lib. bdg.)
  ISBN-13: 978-0-531-20932-5 (pbk.)   ISBN-10: 0-531-20932-6 (pbk.)
  1. Oviraptor—Juvenile literature. I. Title. II. Series.
  QE862.S3M33165 2012
  567.912—dc23   2011033315

SCHOLASTIC, CHILDREN'S PRESS, ROOKIE READ-ABOUT®, and associated logos are
trademarks and/or registered trademarks of Scholastic Inc.

1 2 3 4 5 6 7 8 9 10 R 21 20 19 18 17 16 15 14 13 12

Photographs © 2012: Courtesy of Dinosaur Resource Center, Woodland Park,
Colorado: 28, 29; Getty Images/De Agostini Picture Library: 26, 10, 31 top right;
Luis V. Rey: 16, 20; National Geographic Stock/John Sibbick: cover, 6; Photo
Researchers: 4 (Christian Darkin), 18, 24, 25, 31 bottom left, 31 bottom right
(Julius T. Csoyonyi); The Image Works/The Natural History Museum: 8, 9,
14, 22, 31 top left.

TABLE OF CONTENTS

4

MEET THE OVIRAPTOR

The Oviraptor (OH-vuh-rap-tur) lived millions of years ago. Scientists are not sure what the Oviraptor looked like.

The Oviraptor ate lizards and other small animals.

The Oviraptor probably had feathers on its body. But it could not fly.

10

The Oviraptor had a head with a triangle shape on top. It is called a crest.

HOW BIG?

The Oviraptor was shorter than an adult man. It weighed about the same as a goose. It was as long as a couch.

14

DINNERTIME

The Oviraptor had a beak like a bird. It did not have teeth.

How did the Oviraptor catch lizards? It used its sharp claws.

GOOD PARENTS

The Oviraptor laid its eggs
in nests. It sat on the eggs to
keep them warm.

The Oviraptor took care of the babies. It fed them food from its own mouth.

FIGHTING

The Oviraptor used its claws
to fight.

It also had long back legs.

25

26

It could run fast. It could easily chase its prey.

DINOSAUR BONES

Scientists found Oviraptor bones. They built a skeleton from the bones. It is in a museum.

Can you find the claws on the skeleton? Can you find the long back legs?

TRY THIS! Ask your child if he can recall from the book how the Oviraptor used its claws (to catch lizards; to fight). Go back in the book with your child and compare the parts on the skeleton with the illustrations. This is a fun way to talk with your child about what he just read.

OVIRAPTOR FACT FILE

 The name Oviraptor means "egg thief."

 The Oviraptor's tail stuck out when it walked.

Visit this Scholastic web site for more information on the Oviraptor: **www.factsfornow.scholastic.com**

beak

crest

nest

Oviraptor

Index

Learn More!

You can learn more about the Oviraptor at:

www.nmns.edu.tw/nmns_ eng/04exhibit/permanent/LifeScience/ Age_of_Dinosaur/dino_04.htm

About the Author

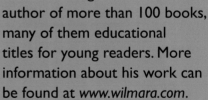

Wil Mara is the award-winning author of more than 100 books, many of them educational titles for young readers. More information about his work can be found at *www.wilmara.com*.